FABIANA ATTANASIO

Mythographic

COLOR AND DISCOVER

Frozen Fantasies

AN ARTIST'S COLORING BOOK OF
WINTER WONDERLANDS

CASTLE POINT BOOKS
NEW YORK

T0041863

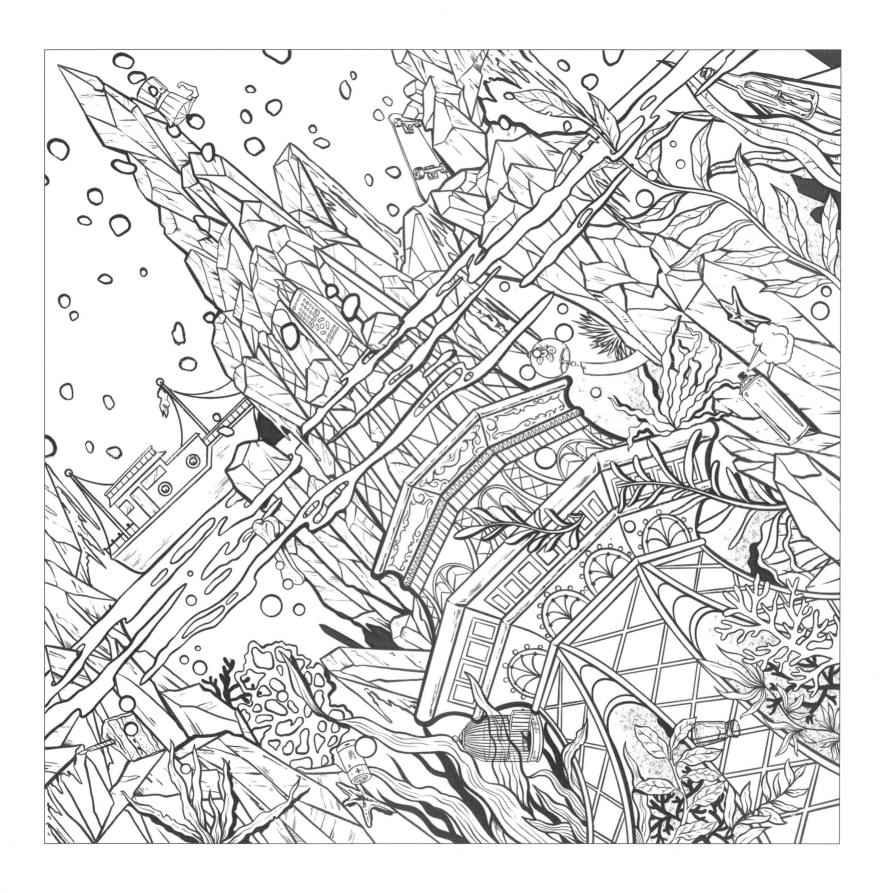

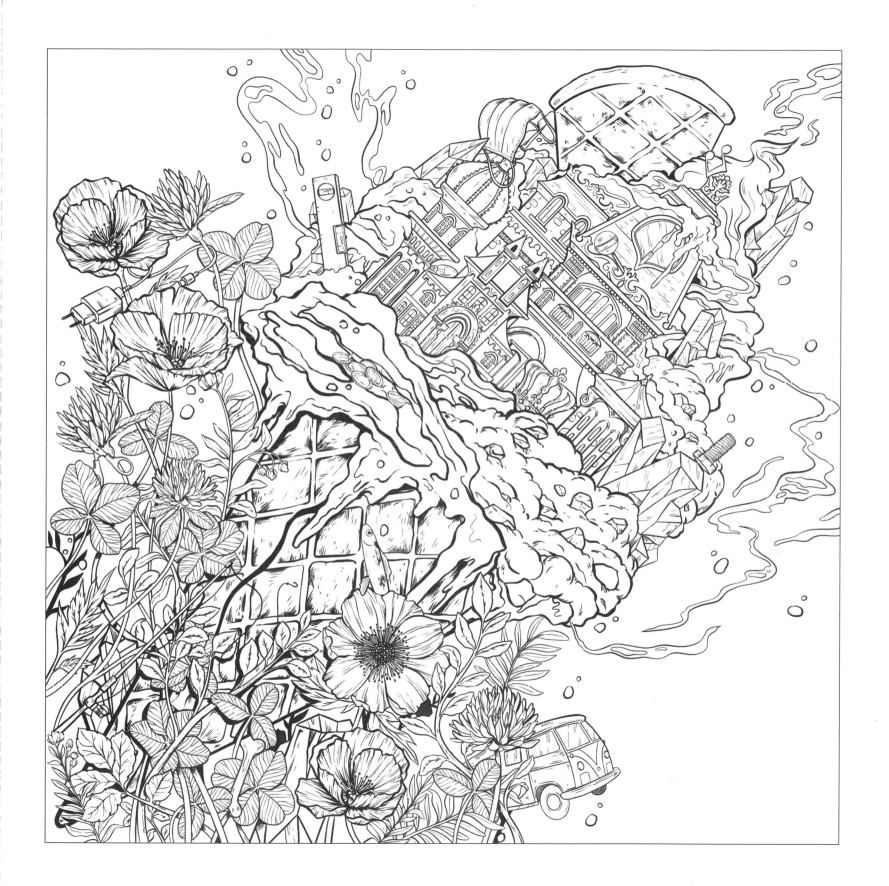

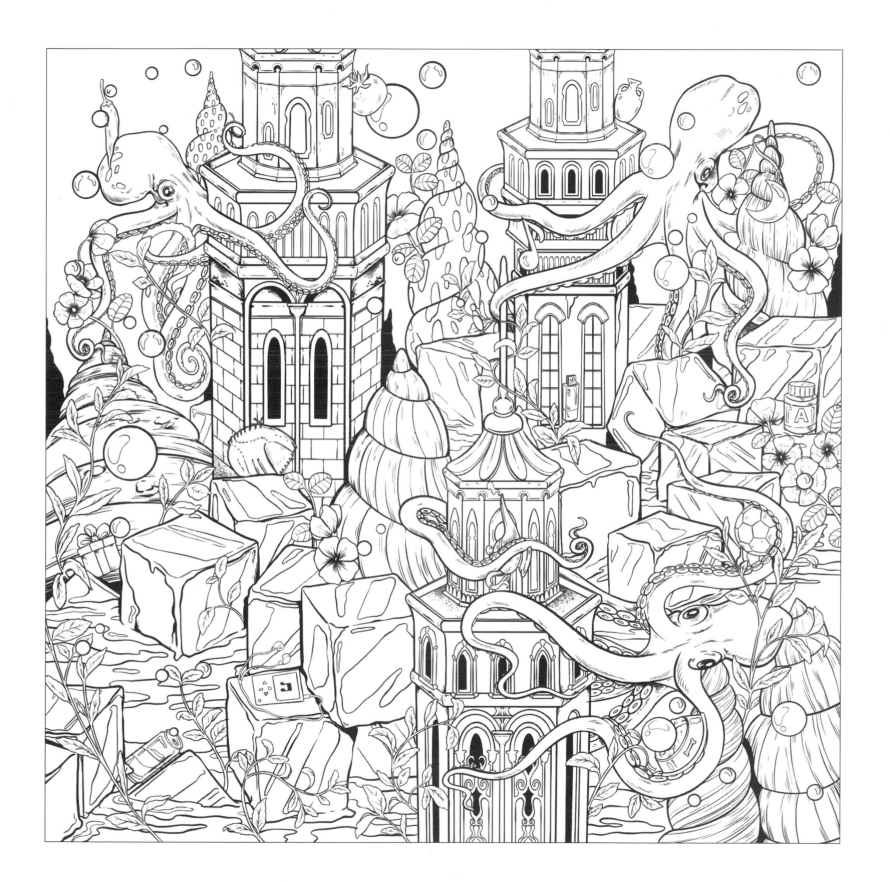

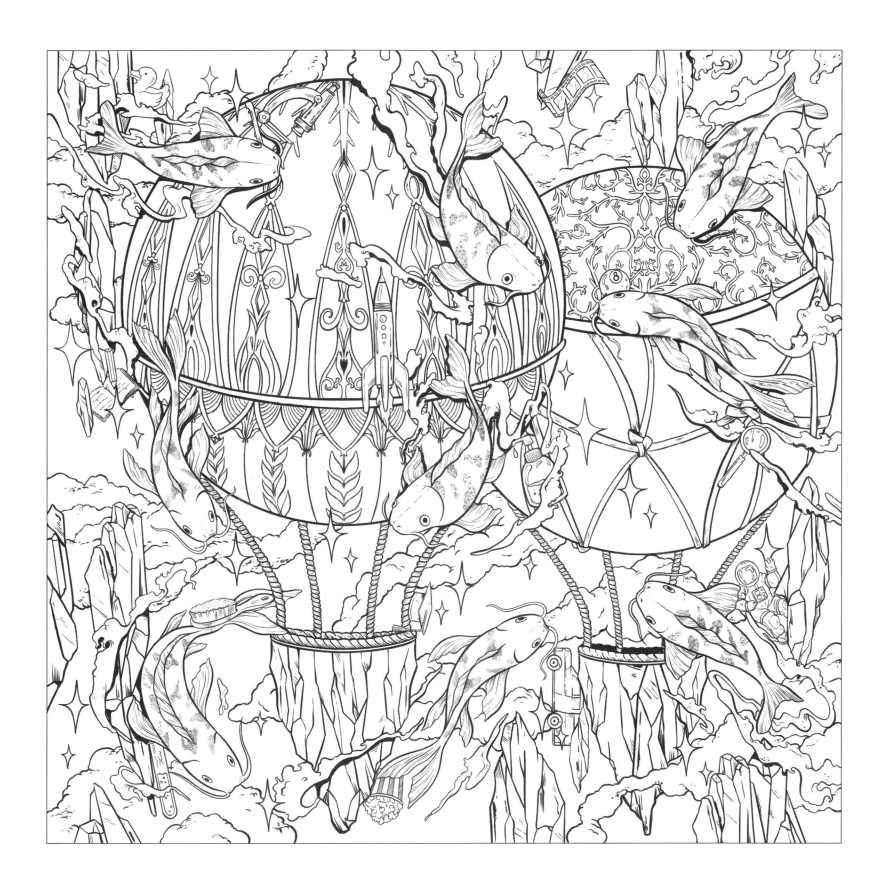

HIDDEN OBJECTS REVEALED

COVER

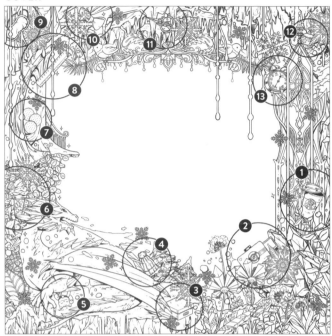

1 Coffee Cup 2 Polaroid Camera 3 Cardboard Box 4 Winter Hat
5 Lucky Cat 6 Ice Cream Cone 7 Cookies 8 Ruler 9 Sleeping Mask
10 Bow 11 Scissors 12 Christmas Ornament 13 Alarm Clock

SWORD

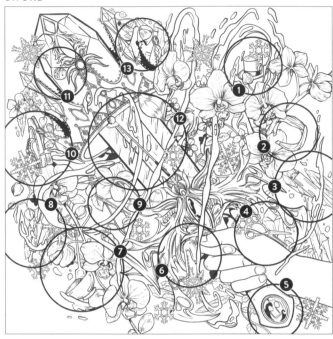

1 Top Hat 2 Headband 3 Lighter 4 Scissors 5 Music Note
6 Saxophone 7 Hair Dye Set 8 Rolling Pin 9 Bobby Pin 10 Shoe
11 Dice 12 Golf Club 13 Shirt

VESSEL

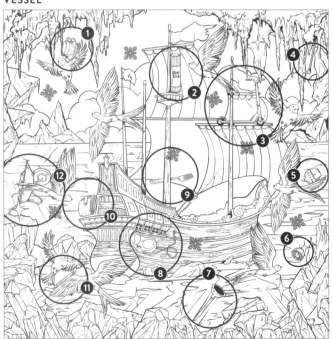

1 Coffee Cup 2 Glue Stick 3 Scooter 4 Match 5 Kitchen Timer
6 Bowl of Soup 7 Plunger 8 Leash 9 Fork 10 Wallet
11 Pencil 12 Wheelbarrow

ARIES

1 Tack 2 Oscar 3 Sneaker 4 Blackboard 5 Skeleton Key
6 Nunchaku 7 Hand Sanitizer 8 Music Note 9 Magnifying Glass
10 Pen 11 Bowling Pin 12 Hourglass 13 Fork 14 CD

SNOWFLAKE FAIRY

1 Witch's Hat 2 Mushrooms 3 Roller Skate 4 Compass 5 Pencil
6 Music Note 7 Match 8 Ladle 9 Football 10 Sack
11 Magnifying Glass 12 Shirt 13 CD Case 14 Diamond

LEVIATHAN

1 Rubber Duck 2 Tweezers 3 Screw 4 Turnip 5 Electric Toothbrush
6 Sword 7 Skeleton Key 8 Smartphone 9 Bolt 10 Pencil
11 Spinning Wheel 12 Paper Airplane 13 Flip-Flops

PHOENIX WIND

1 Clapperboard 2 Pencil 3 Headphones 4 Sunglasses
5 Lawn Mower 6 Paper Airplane 7 Scissors 8 Multi-Sided Dice
9 Fork 10 Broom 11 Fishhook 12 Nail 13 Tube of Paint

ICY CHAMELEON

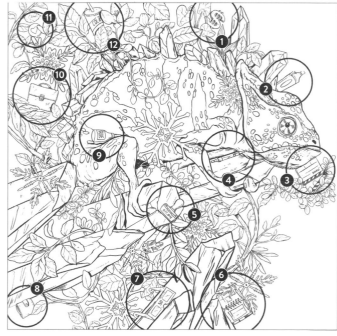

1 Dollar Sign 2 Highlighter 3 Clapperboard 4 Felt-Tip Pen
5 Decorative Stamp 6 Diary 7 3D Glasses 8 Wallet
9 Glue 10 Briefcase 11 Heart Balloon 12 Cola

CASTLE

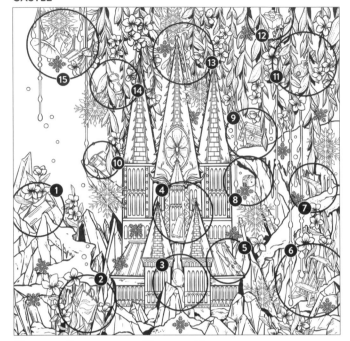

1 Lighter 2 Shopping Bag 3 Balloon 4 Toothbrush Set
5 Clothespin 6 Rocking Chair 7 Boomerang 8 Dice
9 Treasure Chest 10 Roll of Film 11 Key 12 Toy Brick 13 Cane
14 Pepper Grinder 15 Gramophone

DRAGON

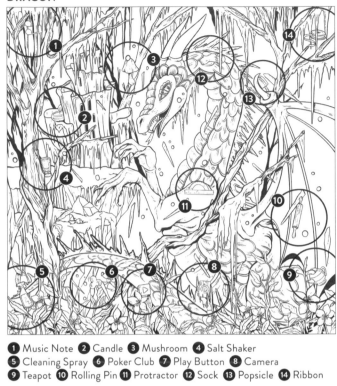

1 Music Note 2 Candle 3 Mushroom 4 Salt Shaker
5 Cleaning Spray 6 Poker Club 7 Play Button 8 Camera
9 Teapot 10 Rolling Pin 11 Protractor 12 Sock 13 Popsicle 14 Ribbon

SNOW QUEEN

1 Pennant 2 Saw 3 Starfish 4 Makeup Palette 5 Shoe
6 Tape Measure 7 Slice of Toast 8 Ruler 9 Quiver
10 Rabbit Plush 11 Juice Box 12 Diving Fins 13 Nail 14 Bolt
15 Newspaper

PEACEFUL PALACE

1 Duster 2 Fishbone 3 Toy Brick 4 Banana 5 Smoking Pipe
6 Clothespin 7 Dice 8 Puzzle Piece 9 Scissors 10 Perfume 11 Bow

NEPTUNE

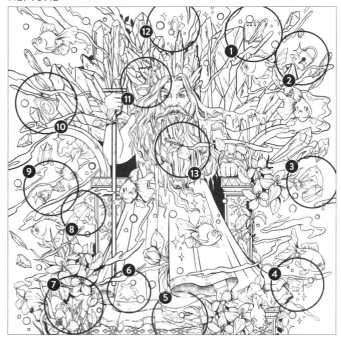

1 Calendar **2** Lock **3** Bag **4** Candle **5** Scoop of Flour
6 Puzzle Piece **7** Tooth **8** Skirt **9** Hourglass **10** Washing Machine
11 Ladle **12** Dish **13** Turnip

THE GREAT ICE MONKEY

1 Sneaker **2** Valentine Chocolates **3** Mouthwash **4** Kitchen Knife
5 Pencil **6** Game Boy **7** Toothbrush **8** Jolly Roger **9** Paintbrush
10 Screw **11** Yarn

GRIFFIN

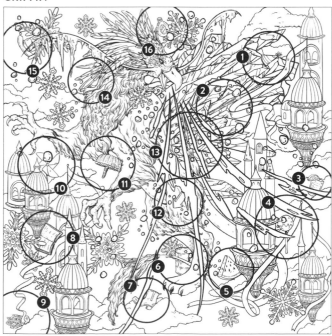

1 Party Hat **2** Match **3** Lemonade **4** Lollipop **5** Watermelon Slice
6 Oil Drum **7** Boot **8** Book **9** Potted Plant **10** Pinwheel **11** Basket
12 Arrow Sign **13** Broom **14** Tweezers **15** Cowboy Hat **16** Detergent

TOWER

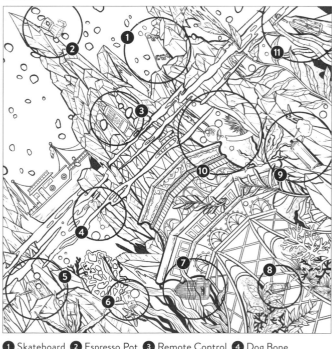

1 Skateboard **2** Espresso Pot **3** Remote Control **4** Dog Bone
5 Slice of Cake **6** Battery **7** Birdcage **8** Salt Shaker **9** Spray Can
10 Wind Chime **11** Message in a Bottle

ICE AND MUSHROOMS

1 Nigiri Sushi **2** Bolt **3** Pendant **4** Whistle **5** Feather Pen **6** Cleaver
7 Chess Piece **8** Necktie **9** Harp **10** Cap **11** Cappuccino **12** Toothpaste

ABANDONED PLACE

1 Set Square **2** Onigiri Rice Ball **3** Key Chain **4** Screw **5** Fossil
6 Tomato Can **7** Shell **8** Stereo **9** Slingshot **10** Torii Gate
11 Fishing Net **12** Magic Wand **13** Book

THE PRINCESS AND THE BEAR

1 Kayak **2** Pillow **3** Makeup Brush **4** Telephone **5** Power Strip
6 Bottle **7** Pencil Sharpener **8** Tea Bag **9** Shirt **10** Globe **11** Hook
12 Slice of Cake **13** Movie Camera **14** Milk Carton

VOYAGE

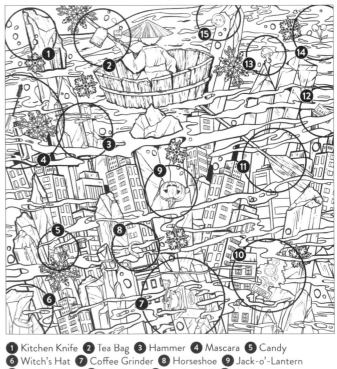

1 Kitchen Knife **2** Tea Bag **3** Hammer **4** Mascara **5** Candy
6 Witch's Hat **7** Coffee Grinder **8** Horseshoe **9** Jack-o'-Lantern
10 Car Freshener **11** Paintbrush **12** Credit Card **13** Mushroom
14 Cherries **15** Button

POLAR

1 Plague Mask **2** Toy Train **3** Baby Bib **4** Christmas Tree Topper
5 Skateboard **6** Cannon **7** Gear **8** Calendar **9** Magnet **10** Baseball
11 Colander **12** Honey Jar

FUTURE

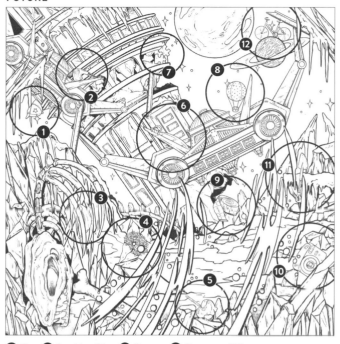

1 Cap **2** Smoking Pipe **3** Banana **4** Bouquet of Flowers
5 Caramel Apple **6** Cutlass **7** Puzzle Pieces **8** Hot Air Balloon
9 Measuring Tape **10** Polaroid Camera **11** Shovel **12** Bicycle

MOTHS

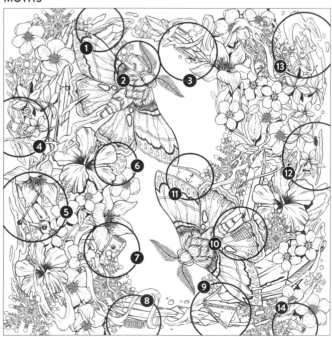

1 Tweezers **2** Scuba Goggles **3** Match **4** Anchor **5** Scooter
6 Easter Egg **7** Electric Shaver **8** Metal Slinky **9** Banner **10** Pan Flute
11 Sailor's Hat **12** Mascara Wand **13** Treasure Map **14** Erlenmeyer Flask

LANTERN GLOW

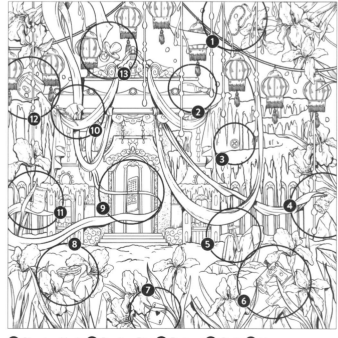

1 Sleeping Mask **2** Bowling Pin **3** Button **4** Cork **5** Hammer
6 Sewing Machine **7** Playing Card **8** Peanut **9** Remote Control
10 Flag **11** Receipt **12** Fish Bowl **13** Pacifier

ICE CREAM

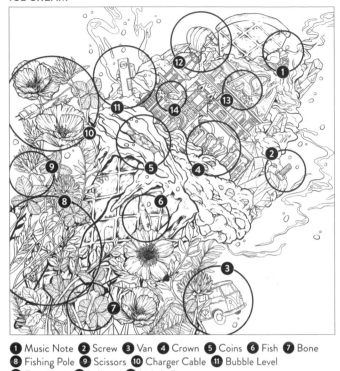

1 Music Note 2 Screw 3 Van 4 Crown 5 Coins 6 Fish 7 Bone
8 Fishing Pole 9 Scissors 10 Charger Cable 11 Bubble Level
12 Face Mask 13 Lollipop 14 Lightbulb

DESERT OF ICE

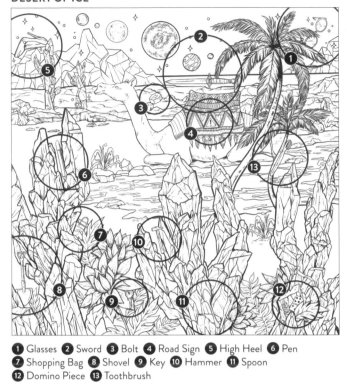

1 Glasses 2 Sword 3 Bolt 4 Road Sign 5 High Heel 6 Pen
7 Shopping Bag 8 Shovel 9 Key 10 Hammer 11 Spoon
12 Domino Piece 13 Toothbrush

WHALE

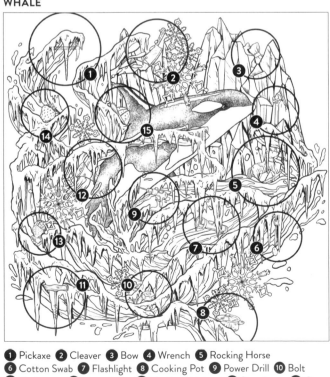

1 Pickaxe 2 Cleaver 3 Bow 4 Wrench 5 Rocking Horse
6 Cotton Swab 7 Flashlight 8 Cooking Pot 9 Power Drill 10 Bolt
11 Corkscrew 12 Megaphone 13 Medieval Helmet 14 Strawberry 15 Cap

OCTOPUS REIGN

1 Ceramic Pot 2 Moon Pendant 3 Vitamin Bottle 4 Soccer Ball
5 Dog Bowl 6 Magic Lamp 7 Mp3 Player 8 Soda Can 9 Gift
10 Baseball Glove 11 Pepper 12 Tomato 13 Music Note 14 Flash Drive

PEACOCK GARDEN

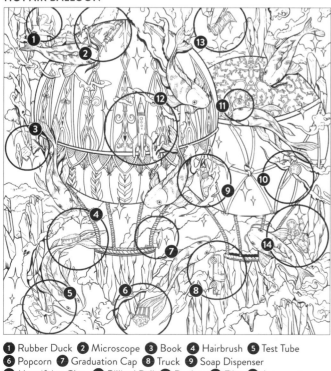

1 Sailor's Hat **2** Beach Ball **3** Bow and Arrow **4** 2nd Place Sash
5 Dynamite **6** Taco **7** Rake **8** Suitcase **9** Target **10** Glasses
11 Watering Can **12** Lighter **13** Treasure Map

POND

1 Toothbrush **2** Safety Pin **3** Notebook **4** Star Bag **5** Diamond
6 Chewing Gum **7** Teddy Bear **8** Knitting **9** Spool of Thread
10 Coffee Beans **11** Socks **12** Musical Triangle **13** Sponge **14** Button

HOT AIR BALLOON

1 Rubber Duck **2** Microscope **3** Book **4** Hairbrush **5** Test Tube
6 Popcorn **7** Graduation Cap **8** Truck **9** Soap Dispenser
10 Magnifying Glass **11** Billiard Ball **12** Rocket **13** Film **14** Astronaut

SNAIL SHELL CITY

1 Tack **2** Dress **3** Hand Mirror **4** UFO **5** Pencil **6** Arrow Symbol
7 Lantern **8** Wooden Torch **9** Telescope **10** Dagger **11** Wheelbarrow
12 Espresso Pot **13** Croissant

MERMAID

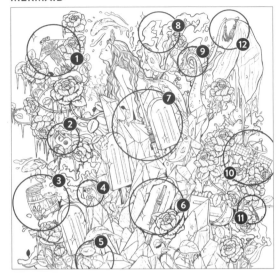

1 Chinese Kite 2 Tape Dispenser 3 Barrel 4 Gears
5 Beach Ball 6 Ink Pen 7 Lightsaber 8 Lightning Bolt
9 Candy Cane 10 Satellite 11 Screw 12 Earrings

LABYRINTH

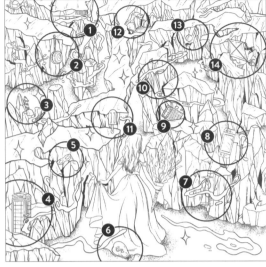

1 Comb 2 Yo-Yo 3 Firework 4 Phone Booth
5 Ball Mask 6 Sack of Gold 7 Bicycle Pump
8 Game Console 9 Calculator 10 Drinking Straw
11 Popsicle 12 Erlenmeyer Flask 13 Music Note 14 Kite

ON THE TREE

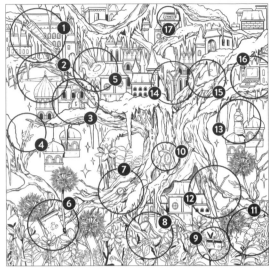

1 Saw 2 Baseball Bat 3 Trophy 4 Airplane
5 Flamingo Pool Float 6 Recycling Bin 7 Watch
8 Duffel Bag 9 Credit Card 10 Alarm Clock
11 Ice Cream Cone 12 Ironing Board 13 Plastic Bottle
14 Zipper 15 Swimsuit 16 Laptop 17 Ticket

SLEEP

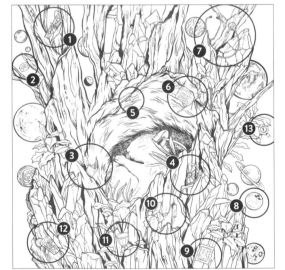

1 Clothespin 2 Bolt 3 Lighter 4 Wheel 5 Tack
6 Knitting 7 Stethoscope 8 Bowling Ball 9 Portrait
10 Paint Roller 11 Bongo Drum 12 Iced Drink
13 1st Place Sash

CASTLE OF BOOKS

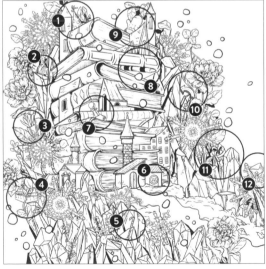

1 Party Hat 2 Thimble 3 Aloe Plant 4 Measuring Tape
5 Candy Cane 6 Button 7 Chess Piece 8 Crayon
9 Oven Mitt 10 Arrow Symbol 11 Gift 12 Envelope

PENGUINS

1 Tank Top 2 Tongs 3 Boxing Glove 4 Paint Bucket
5 Book 6 Sailboat 7 Desk Lamp 8 Pencil
9 Skeleton Key 10 Lollipop 11 Sneaker 12 Rubber Eraser

FOX

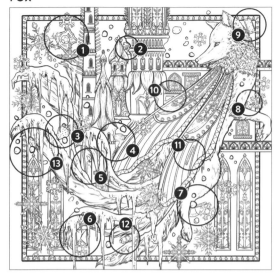

1 Police Badge 2 Mushroom 3 Strawberry
4 Smoking Pipe 5 Candle 6 Envelope 7 Axe
8 Spinning Top 9 Smartphone 10 Set Square 11 Pencil
12 Tube of Paint 13 Crystal Pendant

BIRDS

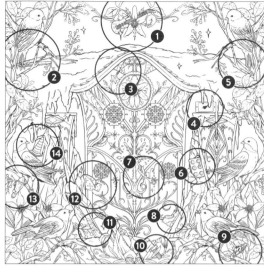

1 Electric Guitar 2 Hair Straightener 3 Star Pendant
4 Smartphone 5 Pen 6 Toy Brick 7 Scissors 8 Shoe
9 Planet 10 Screw 11 Lipstick 12 Kokeshi Doll
13 Lightbulb 14 Traffic Cone

ELK

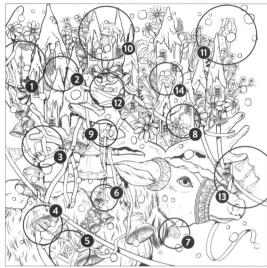

1 Pendant 2 Candle 3 Hat 4 Paint Palette
5 Birthday Card 6 Question Mark 7 Coin
8 Shopping Bag 9 Puzzle Piece 10 Pajamas 11 Bed
12 Candy 13 Scale 14 Steering Wheel

JELLYFISH

1 Safety Pin 2 Football 3 Flip-Flops 4 Lightbulb
5 Spool of Thread 6 Music Note 7 Diamond Ring
8 Journal 9 Bolt 10 Question Mark 11 Apple Core
12 Binder Clip 13 Candy 14 Pencil

SNOW GUARDIAN

1 Necktie 2 Music Note 3 Paintbrush 4 Pen
5 Battery 6 Chess Piece 7 Headband 8 Fries
9 Corkscrew 10 Scroll 11 Tennis Racket

Discover more of Mythographic

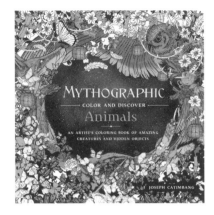
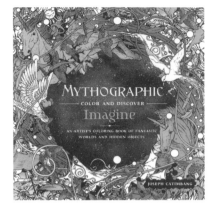
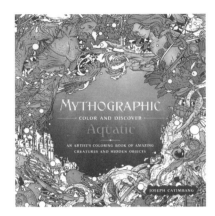

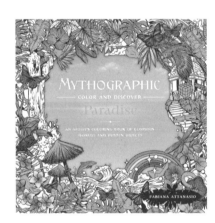

MYTHOGRAPHIC COLOR AND DISCOVER: FROZEN FANTASIES.
Copyright © 2021 by St. Martin's Press.
All rights reserved. Printed in Canada. For information,
address St. Martin's Press, 120 Broadway, New York, NY 10271.

www.castlepointbooks.com

The Castle Point Books trademark is owned by Castle Point Publishing, LLC.
Castle Point books are published and distributed by St. Martin's Press.

ISBN 978-1-250-27112-9 (trade paperback)

Cover design by Young Lim
Edited by Monica Sweeney

Our books may be purchased in bulk for promotional, educational, or business use.
Please contact your local bookseller or the Macmillan Corporate
and Premium Sales Department at 1-800-221-7945, extension 5442,
or by email at MacmillanSpecialMarkets@macmillan.com.

First Edition: 2021

10 9 8 7 6 5 4 3